et j'ai quelquefois vu
ce que l'homme a cru voir

~ Arthur Rimbaud (French)

and sometimes I have seen
what man thought he saw

~Arthur Rimbaud (English)

the alchemy

of

arbitrary air

by

Kris Ehrnstrom

720 Sixth Street, Box # 5
New Westminster, BC
CANADA V3L 3C5

Title: The Alchemy of Arbitrary Air
Author: Kris Ehrnstrom
Cover Art: by Kris Ehrnstrom
Layout and Editing: Candice James
ISBN 9781774033210 (Print)
ISBN 9781774033227 (Ebook
© 2024 Silver Bow Publishing

All rights reserved including the right to reproduce or translate this book or any portions thereof, in any form except for the use of short passages for review purposes, no part of this book may be reproduced, in part or in whole, or transmitted in any form or by any means, electronically or mechanically, including photocopying, recording, or any information or storage retrieval system without prior permission in writing from the publisher or a license from the Canadian Copyright Collective Agency (Access Copyright)

Library and Archives Canada Cataloguing in Publication

Title: The alchemy of arbitrary air / by Kris Ehrnstrom.
Names: Ehrnstrom, Kris, author.
Identifiers: Canadiana (print) 20240458117 | Canadiana (ebook) 20240458818 | ISBN 9781774033210
  (softcover) | ISBN 9781774033227 (Kindle)
Subjects: LCGFT: Prose poems.
Classification: LCC PR6105.H76 A79 2024 | DDC 821/.92—dc23

Part 1 – Appearance / 9

Part 2 – Water / 49

part 1: *appearance*

THE INTERWEAVING OF PRIOR THINGS. Wishes have sometimes been made in regard to you not belonging anywhere. You might have wished to utter words, unaware of their motivation, just to say them, *throw them on our instant surroundings* and watch them break the connection to former distrusts in shapes. A non-hyphenated room trying to structure itself, *in procession*. A city there, cased in glass, fluid, mutable behind the surface of early memories

       it will get worse, *she says stacking up metaphors*, until garments are completed, hyphens are laid to rest and distinctions between inequal things are smoothened like a dolphin's skin, slipping right out of time and correspondence. SEEING TRUTH REDUCES ENTROPY, even textual: *awake in the lack of correspondence*, so precise, as if I was dreaming that I was writing poetry, weaving the reader in writing, about me writing as if I was awake, writing

TIME, *here*, occupies a privileged position, a well that never dries out: *a reeve in any given correlation*, if beingness takes place in water. The patience contained in a message, equally encased, that reaches its destination in time isn't present in its voice, apropos lovemaking analogous to speaking, *speech*: It is a train station that wants to free itself from its all to well-known tracks. Stillness precedes movement, she says, even if a shadow sometimes seems to claim a lasting pattern. Sun followed without coherent markers; we only really touch the ground where we once walked. THE WRITER IS THERE, *and yet not*, writing, but uncertain if the text is writing itself: this is the place of death and resurrection and masking with the other, she says, a meditation on two lovers that only ever just met

Texture, textual, fabric, fabricated... BUT METAPHOR ESCAPES METAMORPHOSIS: *is it enough to absolutely live in words*, inside them? Clothed in text. The letters are stiches, *dolphins breaching and diving*, weaving, formative and shiny (to say the least) and our surroundings seem to derogate regardless, in orderly fashion towards prepositions, small discontinuations of bearing, here *places*: the edge of a mountain shall become the last metaphor if the page is to be likened with snow. WHITE AS MIND, *cold as a made bed*, unnoticed. The book might be a cool face, she says, but if not relativity, what else is there to explore? My life is your life, that is how you create me. An image of you through me as relative your image. Birch tree leaves befallen only when there is ground around their autumn. An edge of a mountain that only takes place in bed. A wind-still assertion behind every wind, every way. *Can we sacrifice metaphor and keep poetry intact?* All roads lead to Rome, they say, but beyond that interwoven edge is but you, coming, arriving in the coming of you. A WATERFALL

OF BRIEF IMAGE, now that we find ourselves in the instances of things befallen. That is why I remain seemingly distant, she says, *there are minds until which certain images retain absolute priority*, and I need to explore the transparent light of other without falling too much, the mapping of language will lead me there and then preferably to you, since these words just became yours

If you think I'm looking for God, as a means to absolutely remain, here, *IN YOU*, in this subversive act of sex, eat, sleep, repeat, then you've doubtfully read lines of mine: even the libertine (with the risk of analogically staining our thing) is in desperate need of the other, *he is the slave of his object*. But it is right there, you see. In the absence of absolute form, *in*. You just know it too well, she says, that's why you forgot how to know. The great in-between. The old land never not newly discovered. Canyons of air. Fields of beautiful nothing. But in relation to what? Nothing cannot be more or less. The middle is always furthest away, and closest. Nothing new under sun ripe sayings, hiding. Even letters unwritten fall back into white page, sleeping, acting out the same subversion. Again: nothing ordinary has made these surprises definite; heaven just as substantial behind words such as *day*, *clouds* and *nacre*, *shimmering echoes*. I can already return to a beginning already in search of me, she says, since the act itself constitutes the future remembered. *Here?*, autumn skin, the window slightly opened, a cool breeze across an all to warm bed. Perhaps the flow of your hips, laying naked on the side – there's *room* in this image, not nothing

We need to own what we forgive. Validate the shape of emotion, hold it like a pale blue sky in our hands and release the wideness to its shapeless desire. I wished I wished many things, she says, that my mind was a complex mesh of algorithms and apocalyptic solutions. Something intricate, exclusive, something to paint an author's room with. But all I want seems so sententiously contained in the word my narrative vitally circulates. PAGE: White, whitening, whiteness, *witness*... A book written around a word, but nonetheless addressing page. The French have always scoffed at etymology, she says, and Inger Christensen dreamt about dreams seen before ever being dreamt but the ontological sphere of sun is nonetheless white and fruitful: *never the zinc-white nights so white*, no half-shadows in transparent houses. *Man lives by image alone*, HENCE WHY THEY SING WE ARE NOTHING, LET US BE ALL, in their fast-food soteriology. Here's the modus operandi: maintained, *in vital fitness*, we paint layers of expectations on a truth that's never allowed to dry — the metaphor is still weeping paint, *still wet* – and become second-hand, wither, released to the past and a history and so on

I imagine the poem like a living room, without ceiling, a space hopefully not saturated by inner mess, furniture or further assessments (*ergo*, RIVERS, CLOUDS AND FURNITURE NEED IMAGINARY HABITATS AS WELL). All forms of entropy stutter the subjective, hence its form, but the trees at the end of the street seldom grow sideways. (WILL THIS IMAGE DISSOLVE AS WELL, NOW THAT WE
LIE SIDEWAYS?) My phone number is +46768934041, I've had it, this intercommunicative key, though seasons and seasons, the watercolor ones and the emotive ones. Numbers of me. Is there anything other than chaos to contrast order? Outer control as supposed to inner works – *how foolish am I to precede in the reconquest of self?* We leave the house, we take to water, here in the pitch-dark lake of rural north: "swimming" she says swimming, in some sort of tautological defiance, doing gentle backstrokes, and I don't know if I'm swimming in late summer or swimming when the summer

converged with water, cold. A dull scent
of sweet brooks, soaked waterlilies, your
feet, still wet footsteps along the jetty

FOR THE ORIENTATION OF THE READER: we are now back indoors, in geometrical disposition of the body of room, our aoristic blimp immaterielle. The place: pale walls, stingy, a bed on the oak floor, white sheets pouring down its sides, a handful of books next to the bed, a glass of water, a plant in a glass of water, green, late century windows, tall, a chesterfield couch, disintegrating, a newspaper in her hands, she: lying, leaning back, not leaving. Ironic, she says, how the supposed perception of news, here in hands as supposed to morning, advocates immorality and prioritization of newsworthiness against the background of white pages, the color of righteousness, as if what we did here, mediated, written here on white sheets, could ever be construed with unlawful words. Hence the irony, she said, in the watering down of newsworthiness: inflation connotes loss of value, even in sensation, eating of news and sex. But maybe we are amiss of the colors from now on? Close your eyes and point towards your consciousness, a page in the paper. Ebony pale, culture-deviating deep gray. Paint yourself, move coherent as if space, untouched, and touch only me. Touch me as if I was anything but the headline, go ahead

FOR THE VIEWER: outside the window are birch trees, they relay something, something to elusive to not let be: drinkable sap, curly crowns, pale skin, as if not touched by sunshine, and yet melanin grows out from them. It is in the smallest we find the smallest of the grand, in relation we can open and close, observe ourselves in the galaxy that contains birch trees and blue bell flowers. Along the meadows wave, billowy blue outside. *More more green, its greening and blue.* A last page, adherent to the beginning – a letter bigger than the poem of Creation. Where I remain unknown, the only thing of certainty – *I am* – is the ever so uncertain. Hence the negation of its absence. I leave it there; I never pick the flowers. They must grow with the meadow, signify my untouched everlasting, and include my view within this perpetual makeshift of reoccurring seasons

"The surrounded" negates escape, *as theme*: the inability of escape becomes the metamorphosis, *the escape*. That is why a recognition of beauty, OF *THE ALL* AS THEME, makes it impossible to bring a filter to your lips. Instead, you bring lips to my mouth as a means of change, inescapable transformation. I COULD PAINT YOU WITH MY TONGUE JUST FOR MY PLEASURE, *I don't think you know this*. Once again ethereally uncircumcised, touched beyond senses vis-à-vis senses, *skin*, wet labia, now breathing the same kiss, no longer a veil between perception and what longs to be perceived. Later: *the rest?*, she rhetorically asks, is but a cult and we happen to choose even when we're not choosing, *sometimes*, sometimes eventually winter, stretching its arms towards late autumn weather, as if embracing a tired and completed world: but our whiteness is warm, body warm, weather, seasons between coming and going, newfound rest and overstayed sensualism. Out there: cities nevertheless thawing throughout their transience, still a few months left for an autumn with warmth of its own, with room. *Eventually*, is what we most often await, she says, an independent solution, the whimsical point in the end of an open poem. Thin ripples along the surface of bed and lake, both moving towards surface break *breathe again*, both grasping for air, a light promise, a vibration of still legs trampling water. Enough to limit the moment with the freedom a breath serves

When the circle meets itself, you look yourself in the mirror and place your thoughts in air. How the proposition seems to rest within, in intuition, *subject*: a thin bed of ever undocumented arbitrariness, *games* really, interests. Light skies and dissociating worlds. But from *what?*, she asks, disregarding the symmetry of questions as form. The notion maintains its own arbitrariness, *déjà*-du jour, a twofold encounter with language. ANY CREATURE THAT WITHDRAWS IS PREPARING A WAY OUT, but here I am withdrawing into you. To detach from the ones who unconsciously detach (read: *from beauty*) is preferable, she says. The ones sleeping without sunshine in their dreams, without day inside of night, without beauty as a prior form to life. *And you?*, after the words played their habitual part: you remain air, that's how the sky knows you will enter in-between words

It is said that the world was made for two, but it nevertheless seems to sustain an incalculable mass around the immediate spectrum of emotions, a body without a body, depth. The moon affirms even the ones who sometimes forget that the light of night is the sun in translation, the writings that retells the unavailable anecdote of past days. A light that has gone by, she says, is still a light, even if it is lit in distant rooms. Touch me here, she says, there's light there for me. I see myself. *IT IS SAID THAT IF EVERYTHING WAS KISSED BY FIRE, THE FLAME WOULD BE THE LAST THING REMAINING*, and yet nothing but desire really burns. A lot is said, she says, you can say that again, and the words take flight somewhere, like dandelion seeds, unconscious utterances float silently through an occurring field of moment

It is the eternal inconsistency that eventually consumes us, she says, hyperbole won't save us this time – *providing that the end is actually in the end of the sentence.* Not one with the beginning, with the one not beginning. TO BEGIN
THIS WORLD WITH A NEGATIVE FORECAST, now, since we're essentially talking about weather. Quevedo wrote: *polvo serán mas polvo enamorado*, and I'm ready to die in this soft grave of eiderdown and legs. We tend to easily forget the laws of nature, she says, *how emblematic isn't the affected human?* Such a creature of receptive denial, *denial.* AS IF SHE SPOKE
HER BAD QUALITIES ONTO SURROUNDINGS THAT ARE NOT SUPPOSED TO RETELL THE PAST: when was world not *mirror?* anymore; and they retracted their echo as if untouched. Unaware or not, echoes are faithful to causality. A labyrinth of voiceless traits. We never hold contempt towards anyone but ourselves

For how long can self-denial stay maintained within the manifesting sphere? Light, borders. Matter coming together and consolidating an envelope for the somewhat unwritten letter. *But who is the sender?* now that we share address. From dust you came (remember Quevedo), but first after our mothers' waters and dry proverbs. Her coherent coastlines, a sort of seeing, *sea*, now introducing dialectic antagonists: flowing sand dunes, deserts, dams, *absence*. The old Egyptians sometimes referred to Osiris as a living tree, she says, and here he is, still bearing poetic fruit therearound three thousand five hundred years after. But the trees of this world bear no fruit WITHIN OLD GARDENS; *no trees grown behind death for the ones that do not begin their immortality by dying*

In alignment with the future,

a steady stream of nothing, a plain wilderness is housing our most feared beasts. Either NOT TOUCHED BY ANYTHING *or* TOUCH EVERYTHING: *feel the shape of the sky*, the surface that bears the idea of walls within a room. We tend to appear in tales with plots bigger than what we allow ourselves to hear. A meadow, however, needs both blue bell flowers and pale birch trees to make that swishy sound of sea; if you don't see your growth yet that means you are a tree, if you don't hear it, it is a part of your nature: you will stand there from now on, wind in hair. The sound of stillness, the movement of silence. Tell me, what isn't contained in silence? I'll wait

Can you see the predisposition of pages? How a flow of invisible lines prescribes direction, voice – *paroxysmal*, in the mind: *hidden lines*. The rules are already agreed upon, it is towards them you unconsciously build your rebellion, here even sacrificing poetry for message, linguistic ornaments for substance. Even freedom *in form* needs to be validated by law, every revolution derived from a particular origin *in a still, stagnated perfection*. There is no homogenous expression, she says, this would presume a relative contrast, an ineffectual cause:
A BED OF LEAVES ON A FIELD WITHOUT SHADOWS; I'm holding your hand, somewhere, and its either warm or cold so yes, now I know who you are, from which of these invisible lines your revolution of words can be traced, where in this impecunious autumn we are

The clarity in a hazy day, intentions themselves with incentivized demands on a bodily room. Only clouds, eiderdown duvets and semantic references to hide parts of heaven behind. That which is camouflaging and appropriating becomes requested by transparency, *you ask for time*. WHEN TIME CONTINUES THROUGH ITSELF YOU ASK FOR TIME WITHOUT RESERVATIONS, *additional time for what you don't intend to address*. More sunny days for your sunglasses, more rainy days for your raincoat. You want to live, you really do, *but not live*: not die but not let die the parts of you that don't want to
live

Life in its indefectible concept needs to be offered to all aspects within itself, even sleep. *Sleep now*, sleep within sleep. Fragments of the sender, ambiguously influencing my fidelity. I mingle my darkness with light, even here – in her, in the bundle of legs and time non-designated, *but nonetheless remember stars*. Have we all consequently closed our eyes to far less than dreaming? Did we aim too low in our objects of neglect? Moistened corneas with the sum of abandoned days. I can hear languages outside my window, even sleepwalking they talk. A sociable dream, somewhat unusual in its inconspicuous demands: walk in pace, breathe, partake in ideas.

WOKE IS AN ANECDOTAL REFERENCE, the designator is outside of herself, in a different temporal state. Nobody's flying here, she says, the usual dreams are earthbound: even stars visit sometimes, they walk as well on feet before heaven

Transubstantiation once again: You have a letter to pick up, she says and leaves me to be identified by something infinite, whatever it might be: shapeless or not – it's there. Can you allow yourself to see? Our consolidation prior to numbers, the frame of consonants housing vowels and song. SPOKEN INTO APPEARANCE, *iridescent*. The surroundings that arrange themselves around the whereabouts of our past breath, a language pointing towards trees and symbiotic self-description. A narrative in which waves tumble into the reciprocal loyalty of self, no wave outside mind. The sea is the letter, she says, the body is the envelope, the postage has been validated and the breaking wave is the postman

Nothing is mine, she says, it only travels through me on remarkable days. The ones least visible for the ones looking to install days. *To know something*, you must first embrace it. But you cannot embrace the unknown without knowing your arms, *you therefore embrace yourself* and observe your interaction with nothingness, seeking itself through the content of your remarkable days

After always comes before something, that which preceded the after. The prior ground already somewhat cool before the shadow, a receptive spirit of light before the pages' textual expectation. The words are already written, and your happiness is in conjunction with the presence of page against pen, the rest is written backwards, with the motion of the pen, towards the sky. As such there are destinies weaved in letters in clouds, where once light shimmered through. In the sentencing gaps, firmament scars in the foreground of day. *It really couldn't be worse*, she says, it its phenomenologically fallacious: the value of feelings proper bear no subjective indifference, IT SIMPLY FEELS, *it feels*, and we move ourselves around the cause like words around preconceived days, expecting someone to read us

On route: a toe in the world and a thigh, a hip and a pale belly somewhat naked in the light between right and double-right – in this image we see ourselves in nostalgic morning, the light still eager, still morning. We take a walk to the beach, *something to leave behind*, a toe mark on the beach between exclusive similarities. Foam and flowing gravel. Cold stones slowly walking backwards out of the water like homesick turtles. You've guessed it, this poem is about homesickness, *maybe limerence*, IF YOUR HOME IS SOMEBODY ELSE: one can be unaware of the closeness of heaven to water, *old without ever have grown*, not closer to heaven than water. You need to get your feet wet, she says, and fend off the rhetoric present in arbitrary cities; here, this metaphor denotes *people*, their internal narrative, their city. *Into me you won't get without help from yourself*

WE ARE OUTSIDE, AROUND AND ABOUT THE HOUSE: They have no mutual order, she says, the tiles on the roof that murmurs heaven back up in a puddle of light blue water. See how it flows from the coulisse *up*, taking form and color as it leaves the ground of treetops and architecture. *Map:* NOW WE ARE INSIDE, IN BED. But that which is in-between ought to be objects known, regardless of how much it differs in density, in cultural value. A dialect of the same manifesting idiom:
THE THING INBETWEEN US IS ALSO A THING, *when I move towards you, I always move through air*, even if this thing between us is a rickety bridge of impossible crossing. I turn to water next, she says, after the air between us weighed my heart and I've hovered out of bed like eiderdown feathers or expressive verbs. A few of them at least, the ones escaping the rift. Even here, indoors, my intentions are spiraling towards this light blue surface of ours, a circle around a water mirror. We must remember, she says, remember the function of remembrance

itself: how we also carry the space between disruptions of light, between the shapes that converts sun-language into color, the city's color into something more faded, something gray. I notice the wind instead, gently pushing against my skin with cool fingers, sneaking in through the somewhat opened window like a weathered cat. *Love demands as it prerequisites the concept of a person*, she says and describes the pathway of air moving across body, but just like everything we control must first be released, what we love must also be destroyed, before we are capable to return the love, let it in like the mirage of a cold cat

AT NIGHT. The wind sounds like the ocean and the moon speaks the voice of sunshine in writing, *almost*. A childlike attempt to walk in a parent's imprints, silent steps. CHILDHOOD'S EXCLUSION FROM ANYTHING OTHER THAN PLAY AND MILD WAVES: we all mimic something, she says, the secret is to be aware of the source, not thing, *idea*, not stale appearance, *intention* – if it is and end of a providing sea that rolls through our language, full of oxygen, form and nutrition, or if the textual garden is to euphemized by a desert, beautiful in its own way, *once*, beautiful as an infinite regression. They are both mothers, on each side of the scale. Only a lucid being can look directly at the unmalleable sun of destiny, she says, that's how we know that the desert was once a lover, and that the green is her new novel. Particle to waveform, liquid to solid, her body now dead and deserted under the blanket of night: *STILL MILD WAVES*, this

Aisha, this child interrupted. Limitations or freedom or the freedom of limitations. There is no female solidarity, she says, just sun only to the day awake or moon in-between, voiced by the immovable body of past deeds

MORNING. If a day stands in front of you without demands – *where will you then find your mission?* In her hair, the warm scent of warm woman, or in references alike? The day not yet daily and temperate, still lingering above its comfort, in the claire-obscure corridor of sleep, night, *existential leisure*, extended awayness in phenomena. *The fingers of the right hand wander over the private parts, and the fingers of the left feel the nipples.* Is that all you got from Waldrop? A rhythmic structure of yes to what comes, and I decline, *this is mine*, this thing of ours. 1x1 *is* 1, but the latter: *changed*, different from its historical signifiers: *there is but a retroactive one*, don't be fooled by its semiotic application. The nascent stage, let's keep it simple: HOW WILL YOU FIND YOUR RELATIVITY? *Now that the theme implies La-femme-Un in the backdrop of individuation.* We shall see if you keep a heaven within yourself, she says and seemingly opens my chest from the inside.

… ljus och frisk. Ljus och ofta. Ljus och frisk…

Robertson wrote in the Swedish translation of *The weather*, but here it's leaking acoustics and shiny scales of color. And I feel so much depends on the weather, *so is it raining in your bedroom?* We don't gotta be in love I just needsumbody right now. RED UP TO PURPLE, *wetness*. Clearly not invisible borders. But are they visible for the unconscious perception? The liminal matrix between sleep and still feeling sleep – *the ground in which this poem grows*, beautiful heaven, true heaven, look at me changing. This moment occupies itself, extirpating the oneiric fabric: what is there to further dream about, not that I woke up and found myself in my dream? The collective sentiment, here, between us two – an interior form, vowels inbetween the furniture, SAY GOD SINCE
THE WORD JUST CAME, *the other constant*: figures, bodies, expressions and so on – a light retentive

There is no true story in the world that was birthed out of the world and now reimagines a world. A self-fulfilling act, we either invent titles and perish thereafter or inherit divine appellations and leave: WHEN A PROVINCIAL TRUTH OUTWEIGHS WORLD, THEN REVOLUTION BEGINS, here from bed. *Note!* this is not a reference to Oasis and *Stand by me*, but rather when Jesus tells the sick man to go, and he picks up his bed and goes. Here world ought to be body and body a form that is every form in the world. You believed some things to be true, but they lied to you nonetheless: you can bring *some of it* to the grave, a mantle of *l'air du temps* (wrapped around you as mise-en-scéne, as room, as supposed to breath), dew wet feet, memories bound to emotion. We bury ourselves in this – *this* – or die before, in an arranged conscious death. We bury ourselves softly in this world, the bed is recursive, an image in image: we pick up the image and go

There is a secret we all share
    generalizations in themselves don't
have the integrity to maintain an objective immanence, she says

    who knows? I might find you
on a rainy day

The proletariat is completely subtracted from the sphere of political representation, here verbatim from Badiou, *so now we know that the proletariat deals with the semiotic inhabitants of an unvoluntary soul in practice*, not body alone, seeing the body requires sustenance and we are currently broke. This poverty of ours seems to reduce us to timelessness and symbiosis, she says, since we are currently slipping into a transhistorical existence, timeless perhaps, outside of world. WE PICK WILD CHERRIES AND APPLES; we have been eating wild cherries and apples so now we sweat fruit when we are having sex. This would surely qualify as poetry in some places, she says, even though incorporation can't be reduced to merely a body, *how glorious it might seem*, slim and fruit-scented sweet. BUT WE ARE ALSO DWELLING IN OLD ARISTOCRATIC NEIGHBORHOODS left standing, we float in the wake of the well fed and beautiful streets, *hungry and fed*, because even though our composition now is cherries and apples, she says, man cannot live by bread alone

part 2: *water*

The evening is mild, the ambience of outside room still gentle, winter hesitant in the recalling of memories. Clusters of leaves are hanging from the beech tree by the old university, the lawns around the flowerbeds seem fat and hungover with rainy nights. *How many seasons of despair before the aesthetic anesthetization of existence,* mind, *is vital?* I wonder who built these, all these empty spaces, and where they've been hiding. WHO IS THE *proto*-ARCHITECT? The architextual designer of *womb*, the retroactive genealogist: in order to emerge into open air, we must first look beyond ourselves: *realization*, just look at the word, how beautifully its function here reads together with its lexeme. The qualia of air towards awareness: YOU ARE REALIZING YOURSELF, and the format is meta, since you're already here, in womb air. We always build beautifully to make the space between houses and letters beautiful; we are dealing with the ornaments of page after all, *the alchemy of autumn air*, she said that time air stood in the way and nothing else was seen but nothing but her: *l'air est un grand maigre*, and imitation too is a sort of transformation. But not until there's enough of nothing outside air, I will come to you and leave you at the same time, she says, like a gift and a curse *dissolving*, like the last of a sun on midsummers eve, I will come to your past valuation with neither future nor past

I have already described the city. How one space asserts the other one's autonomy, man from woman, millions of minds beginning in their subjective alienation with body, not mind. Flowers standing on newly blackened asphalt. Water falling from the sky one drop at a time to avoid the rain. I have pointed at angles of meaningless choices, she says, but I've still only just begone. *In order to transform a text, opening the door to the autogenesis of indefinite numbers of mimetic performances, a simple and mechanical gesture might suffice*: STONE, WATER, *arrogance*, the complete reduction of material things, destroying cities as if they weren't echoes of our textual minds. Tear out a few pages, unless you already have, but bear a testimony before you do, so that you don't fall back into nothing: THE PROPOSITION OF NOTHING IS A TEMPORAL FALLACY, she says, NOTHING IN ITSELF IS AN ANECDOTE, *a historical object*. So how can nothing be if it is always a past reference? Even in performance, revised, performed. Never derogate due to tiredness when beginning, she says, because nothing is closer to the end of illusory nothingness than a first step

On the other hand. How poor isn't the assortment of words meant to describe everything, she says. *Meagre* or *everlastingly rich* – LOVE IS THE ONLY KING I SERVE, the light-blue evening will do as my loyal companion, the inside of the frost giants' eye in this here our l'être ensemble. *The qualia of green and rustling of old summer?* Here we are, endlessly strolling about, and you can't help but think about aesthetics. The outer room is on the way somewhere, across the scale and the curve and all sorts of arithmetic analogies: a bed towards the regression of expression itself, now that winter and soul are conveniently accessible as expressions. I close my eyes before the seasons, in ignorance I still see summer nights inside my eyes, still warmth in the brook. A black serpent with fallen leaves as scales. The iron rich water, reeds just like that, like tracks in the scale patterns of a serpent. A body of water surrounded by water, darkness

I wish you saw the world like me, like the accentuation of localism, then I would perhaps get to know myself before it disappears. A day that goes gently into the night, not kicking and screaming against the dying of the light. WHEN I WAS BROKE AND HAD TO SELL MY LIBRARY, THE ANTIQUARIAN GOT HIS HANDS ON MY DYLAN THOMAS COLLECTION WHEN I WASN'T *looking*, a bit stunned by the business-making and the separation. The copy I had bought in Swansea, by the docks (it is at *Antiquary August*, in Stockholm, please get it back for me or even better buy it for yourself, if you get the chance, it's blue and thick) … Here, speaking volumes: a few decades of ebbing rebellion – *what if we go lifetimes without each other's eyes?* The reconciliation of motion and identity: then, before Dylan Thomas, the revolution of heavenly bodies was but the dialogue of being with itself, just as every young dog is the ontological masturbation of a God asexual – *the rebellion adheres to the realm of acci-*

dent and rhapsody, as if the clock sometimes jumps itself out of mechanics, *as if lovers didn't find a moment to escape*

PREPOSITIONS. I haven't begun to think about my thoughts *on* something in a long time, she says, the proposition is too haptic and meta, too architextually generic to not distract with bursts of purposeless sex – *it must remain in withdrawn meditation*, I cannot be aware of white sheets when I'm making love to you, if mind is to be skin, soul is to be lubrication, body is to be sheet or bed. Thought passes through and holds, it retains and reveals, not lays on top of matter like a quilt of late september rain. A floor of cold morning through the window. The morning, however, surrounding and apparently on. The layered spirit of early hours. THE QUICKENING, *quickly seize me*, go straight from sleep to me, awake only like this. Thought is the marriage of spirit and matter, she says, not unlike the mellow ease – *the question* – against the warm answer of a duvet, a bed still lingering in nightly hours. The morning needs a body, just like spirit needs matter to engage in thought, the morning is its body. Otherwise, *unincorporated*, it loses its erotic element. One loves a person, not an abstraction, even in thought. As I make ready to tell this tale to you, methinks I see rocks come rushing to hear me

Nothing is mine, she says, that has already been established. *Remember?* When it passed through my dormant soul and received a voice. *Ergo*: how I retell a universal beauty in a personal day. What I choose to reflect in times of abhorrent ideologies and simmering cities. With what other means can I find what is intended for me? And furthermore, does my search *constitute its absence*? CLOSEST, that which to me lost doesn't become in the destruction of body; and she never had to look far for herself. I am immortal, she says, I know myself, I think. A lamp shaped like a dove, burning continuously, *obviously*, she said once, that's what I am. Clearly designated, in syntax ad nauseum: me, me, me – *the Other*, lost in style and this transformation, stuck in page to the imposed reality of a writer's mind. "The thin fabric of her blouse fluttered like grass at the edge of a fountain ever ready to rise, like the plumage of a pigeon about to fly away", *shut up*, how dare you, when we're talking about style, doves and search for beauty: DIE TO LIVE, *walk down the street with new eyes and leave roses where they grow*, leave them to be unclaimed, nothing in this world, and therefore mine

The mimetic impulse drives us to clean the manifestation. MUTATIS MUNTANDIS, *limit the mess to our own mess*. The mind? I thought we were done addressing that, she says. *Kairos*, some call it, but I am more keen to lean on the occasionalist face: "I enquire as to this health and state of mind, I offer my services without much haggling over details or standing upon ceremony" – it serves as an aesthetic necessity, this quoting culture of hers: pacing half naked across the hollow apartment, book in hands, slipping in and out if irreducible otherness and relational news: HORROR VACUII, the fear of nothingness, if you define yourself as absent lighted, *black*, how can you then be aware of your inability to see your unenlightenment? Life itself, equally irreducible, not known until lived. No single answer lay ahead of its time, she says, we need to first exhaust the love making *baby* to extend our moments. We my darling are real after all, out there we can caricature our involvement, act as an ironic pastiche of good citizens, but in here my sweet,

sweet darling we must never pretend to be dwelling lovers, resting, that which we are: 'tis why I clean, she says, until the day inside will dispose of my journey and I'm ready to write again – *the poem of mind and love rooted in the page like a full grown meadow*, in the foreground of mind, recognizing itself in love. Air and climactic digestion distances what narration requires, soon I can partake again, come again: A TEXTUAL LIVINGROOM OF GRASS AND CURLY BIRCH TREE
CROWNS

We'll put the couch by the lonely pine, she says, *an acquiescence to exist as such*, make a clothing rack of the hanging branch. "… with artistic designs of cherubim you shall weave them… bars of acacia wood… a veil woven of blue, purple and scarlet thread… and covering of dolphin skins above that…" *Is this really IKEA?* I don't really know what lead me here, I must be as clear as possible about that and clear the universal air: THE HUMAN IS LOOKING OUTSIDE HERSELF, echoing back onto her now closed gates. That's it. *On an emphatic note*: Everything is already burning; the earth is already dust, and we are walking in the last memories of one specific moment. It was never cars or factories or recycle bins, *oh the arrogance*, IT WAS ALWAYS GOD and the pharaoh that wants you to blame *him*. Even self-consuming life wants to live, she says, *don't be cruel*, even the illusion of absolute negation needs practice and time

The now is in constant affect to the future we don't remember looking back from

    "*a book writing time we sometimes unintentionally read*: … "The term *pastiche* appeared in France at the end of the eighteenth century in the terminology of painting. It was a transfer of the Italian word *pasticcio*; the term literally meant 'paste' and designated first a mixture of diverse imitations, then a particular imitation." *Palimpsests*, Gérard Genette

ONLY STILLNESS
CAN precede MOVEMENT, *retroactively*. We call this page within it *days*, on it: day and night. Ours is the age of communication, but what happens to our emergent object *fin' amors*, our new Occitania, our Ochrasy – *our dissolving body* – once we are out of touch, *I am still sweating anecdotes*. They make a grave mistake, she says, when thinking it is the body that makes love, au contraire, the body is really in the way, separating, opening, ceasing to be form and becomes the redeeming plow after which soul can both plant itself and be harvested, lose itself

and recover. The sweat is merely parts of soul leaking, don't get lost in the pastiche of body sweetheart, even if you happen to adore mine

THE ECOLOGY OF THE OTHER.
There is no lucidity in the intelligent value that reacts to its surroundings, she says, you need to stop regarding objective rules as personal, *there is no one like the two of us*, no one ready to bear the weight of complete phenomenon, of subject-*sui generis*. Which god can you trust? As if sunshine was only yours in contrast to rain. You always encounter what your meeting wished for, that's why the rain falls differently on wet grass, why the wind welcomes sceneries both at open sea and through your hair, standing by the sea

    tucked into your coat, the sea is a dense table, *o the sea the sea crimson like fire and the glorious sunsets and the syringa bushes in the garden*, the search for merging, the matrix of the other is but completed by water, exiled but now here: LOVE IS A FATE IMPOSED BY THE PAST, but we can't breathe there anymore, *the past*, so we watch the ocean from the shores of our persona to stay alive

SEA. To affirm the currents of conscious streams with your consciousness, she says, *aware of awareness*, and fulfill one's tautological wishes: *I am that I am that I am… and I'm drowning in being*, in I am, swimming, regardless how merciless the sea gets when I let go of the ropes; and she catches them again, here the ropes are synonymous with social material, maybe *looks*. Hedenius assumed that the experience of beauty was a non-propositional intuition, she says, but I am nonetheless aware of that the way you're looking at me now constitutes my beautiful disposition: *your eyes are in a state of affairs*, where I am standing newly out from water, wet and tightly composed. *How does hard naked nipples transform from definition and etiology to pure image?* Goosy bumps and blueish lips. We must detach from this here beach, *obviously*, and make our way indoors to not represent anything, TO KEEP THE CONTENT DETACHED FROM REALITY, because the moment your image of me is that or this, *the moment you with prejudice know who I am*, then the apparition of my naked body as image, here, newly bathed in admiration and cold Nordic water, seizes to be pure and the contemplation moves from metamorphosis to metaphor, and you remember what we said about caricaturing ourselves: THAT IS MEANT FOR THE OTHERS, the ones metaphorically performing life, not living. We must paint the invisibility in allegory and go home again, doors behind doors and back, closed worlds within words. The bed feels new again, we feel new: your feet tucked into the duvet, the window gap now closed towards the light autumn. *You wonder how perception could ever dress this world*; you fear that it is exactly that fear that will dress your perception with this world. Hence why you detach, to stay in the pure image, to stay here as if this moment was world

There are clothes hanging from the pine-tree rack that I can't part myself from.
MEMORIES ARE ALL AROUND US, *spoken into water*, water in translation becomes air. We inhale memories, clothing fibers and befallen stardust. *In this body soon ours*: surroundings not yet formerly obligated to create new memories, not yet bestowed with homophonic echoes, uniform in sound, sighs and moans. Jesus praised the man that ate a lion, cursed the man that was ate by the same. But here I am, *eating you*. Does that make me a woman? I am food in that sense, she says, and we must let someone else get the chance to fall in love with clothes we once wore, to abstract new costumes from memories. *To only face autumn with one's face, hands.* Catharism was said to condemn matter, but here I am, still in clothes, *possibly unbound*: love is not a post-mortem joy, but reserved for us, in body, that stood the test of ultramundane time,

DISREGARDED ALL THE SHALLOW NOICES, and found the place, that emergent place between true

lovers consuming and making mnemonic sounds: *falling in and out of the recognition of self through the other*, one single long memory, recurring, that I only discover and remember in time in
variations of weather, seasons of her

LINGUISTIC TRACES. When the actual writing has commenced and begun its movement, the demand of time descends on the words. We only travel towards immortality in the end, she says, through loops of amnesia and reprised images. Hegel critiqued Kant because he thought that he turned the eye into the subject of knowledge, *but I cannot help to see you*, written: the lines of the poem becomes a rope, you remember it, *the rope from the water right?*, the mooring-rope: HOLD ON WHEN YOU REALIZE THAT DARKNESS DOESN'T ONLY REPROVE A FUMBLING, *now that I'm trying to know you in words* – it darkens across all verbs, even the somewhat made up ones: *even-revolving*, *anamnesis-blue*, *ocean-walking*, INDIGO-SKIES? I'm uncertain of the terminology

IN VESTIGES: *darkness is closest to itself*, total light is closest to darkness but furthest away from itself, the middle both furthest away and closest

an ambient twilight, diluted and entirely moderate

Light is also water, water is skin. There's a dual signification in this matter, she says, since sex is really the prior escape from the perfect reality of the unreal-real, read: GOD, *before man* and matter, but from what standpoint do we predicate escape? From ourselves, the leaping away from persona, or towards ourselves, diving in? Seeing you are the lake and I'm indirectly swimming in the shine of myself

CORRESPONDENCE. It is probably in the bookshelf, she says and points towards what we suppose of forest. Hinting of trees and semiotics. Like right for left, still against any self-denying movement, *THE LINGUISTIC REALM STILL REFERENCES A PRIOR THOUGHT*, don't have us tumbling down into speculation, we are not the only ones thinking, certainly not the highest. Even trees need to take a first step before we, *as tree*, walk towards the completion of sentences, she says, and… *when is enough?* Of gathered materials and linguistic mappings, before mind has gathered enough material to advocate a change according to cells and freedom. BEFORE A TREE DIES IT LEAVES ALL ITS NOURISHMENT AND ALL ITS SCHEMATIC INFORMATION TO NEIGHBORING TREES, *this is called writing*. But in the poetic oeuvre of trees, there is no separation among trees, *there is but one religion*, also written. The devil will eventually try to hide behind prestigious elements, she says, like community, equality, love and religion; *and the trees will judge them*, with death, titled and raging with the utmost stillness in empty pages

TEXTURE. Substance without nerve endings, *even air filled*. Geometrical patterns, ethereal particles breaking unnoticed against skin. Something spoken across the sea, perhaps a sonnet, *might still remain in same air*, air touching your skin in wind. We are still breathing live examples like Bach's Adagio in D Minor, she says, *the world we don't see is still there*, changed, remaining, baptized by our ignorance but somehow known. The second element here, *knowing*, is polemic in nature once it is construed with beingness. But my being is still moved by Bach – *by past physics*, she says, WHICH MEANS THEY CAN NEVER TAKE FROM US ART UNDER THE GUISE OF SOCIAL SCIENCE AND DEFINITION; don't try to intimidate me with trivialities, we just told you, *some things are immortal* & everywhere. What I'm trying to say is that the good times never die, *so leave them alone*. Back to the basics, she says: nothing contains more than all-fashioned-matter, nothing is everything. We simply observe the right things but with wrong names, with eyes seduced by angles. But it is in the surrounding space that preferences are truly granted, the light-blue heaven that makes for an admirable architecture, it is the ether around you – *that transparent mold* – freeing your silhouette to beauty, to me. WE ALWAYS OBSERVE IN UNCONCIOUS CONTRAST TO *assumed* NOTHING, and expect everything from the object when buildings, fountains, bodies in wonder points our assumption back to itself, *to nothing*. As wished. Only in symmetry shapes reprove each other, she says, remember that when the day seems meaningless, *why heaven is called heaven even though you cannot hold it in your hands*

An unsubstantiated calmness admits the situation, that's what you're objecting to. ADMIT IT, YOU LACK THE DEICTICS FOR PEACE, the *locale*. A habit in something without demands, and the resting mind/body becomes unaccustomed. What is the cost of harmony? The negation of capitalism, *is that enough for you*, sweetheart, when you can't even beat your own conditioning: WITH WHAT MEANS WILL *eternity* DEMAND REDEMTION? Do clouds expect a blank blue sky from their observer, *does the lake ask your hair if its wet enough to meet your image of a poem?* Now, that I've written you into water. This is how I remember Scandinavia: slowly flowing across the dark surface, early fallen birch tree leaves and long glances, *us*: already lighter skin. On the other side of the lake stands the woods, the sun is setting, evening light in your hair, glowing white shimmer, wet with sunshine. These observations are not unfitting for a soul

If the orgasm can be reduced to synthesis, recollection ex symbiosis or whatever, she says, *something of spirit and matter and noema and abridging and photons and adagios and clouds and so on*, then I remain disinclined to further calculate my universe, formulate what I tend to discover without a lamp, as lamp, *a fumbling in darkness for pleasurable darkness*.

DISTANCES ARE IN SOME CASES INTERCEPTED, a coincidence? We now-know-*how* the condition itself ought to feel, behind every layer of worldly resistance, it is there – *we are there*, she says, don't look so surprised. Let go of the sheet, let it take to the autumn sky, give the wind a body of history, our bodies are evaporating there, *see*: OUR DAYS ARE WAVING OVER THERE, *white wrinkly corners*. The wind becomes the spirit of the sheet *in retrospect*, the sheet becomes the body left. They are reuniting now, right after the irreducible mystery got back its universe

CONTEXTURE. *Let's be clear*, she says, all this talk about sheets and flying duvets are merely symbolic of our relationship with the reader: *this texture or fabric keeps us covered*, keeps us interwoven in the allegory of itself and its own assumed reading, THE EPIGRAM OPPOSING THE TEXT ITSELF, *unraveling the reader*. I'm always afraid to lose something, she says, to such an extent that I fear my fears will attract the loss, *a form of double fear*. But what is worth my words in the end? If now fear doesn't change its form other than in the genesis of presence. Nothing is scarier than becoming aware of oneself being alive, and then observing this behemoth of world continue its mechanisms. HENCE WHY WE COVER

OURSELVES IN POETRY, *partly*.

Here the concept of periphery is but toes outside the duvet. But the words themselves? Vowels and consonants are woven together to form syllables, some already words, words form, poetry seizes the occasion, *the reader is dressing*; and so

'twas the tale of how written words became history, here in the phenomenal character of reader. *O morning, why now, cruel to lowers, do you slowly unravel around the world, when another grows warm beneath the coat of words*, BEAUTY IS INCOMPLEX, hence its intrinsic contemplation, and these words I just mentioned never touch infinity with affected incentives (don't worry), *only love*, and love is not the effect of imbalanced things, LOVE IS THE
CAUSE *of language itself*, even misused and fearsome. To replace oneself with a text that is closer than our own: derived from *enduein*, to dress, and, more involving, from *enduma*, clothing (IT
ACTUALLY SIGNIFIES *THE ONE OF THE GARMENT*, the garment signifies body, the clothes of soul *in actu*), and the contextualization of our heart's center, *preferably as heart and mind*, our own. FROM NOW ON FORWARD: text – *heart*, and the voice of the reader – *soul in mirror*, in love. *That is how it touches words*, as space. How it seeks itself between the lines of a poem, *a pulsating space*

for the space, a moment dressed in text and soul; the reader is dressing

Let me paint you a scenario, she says. There. It's done. You are here, that's the impressionistic storyline; *lesson*: THIS IS HOW YOU GET SOMEONE TO WAKE UP: pay attention to the blank page, viscerally, pay attention to your mind, pay attention to the sun or the ambient texture of space within your room. *Now that you are violently here*, try to see past the text or the context of your reading whilst reading, forming the texture of moment. You can't, you're inweaved. THE ART OF WEAVING then, as an artisan activity, here as poetry, *as you engaged in undressing*, produces fabricated borders that protects against suffering, *the insufferable revelation of self*, complete nakedness. You see, she says, YOU SHOULD SEE IT
AS CLEAR AS YOU SEE YOUR OWN EYES WHEN THEY SEE THE ROOM, *me undressing*. Clothes falling cordially onto shiny oak floors, here in a

room gathering light in corners: paintings lined up against the walls, never hanged, a pot with a lemon tree. "The reader then, *born*, unties the voice of self within the fabric of the poem", *this is how she reads beyond the poem*, walls, square meters: the only specific parts, true to the apartments description, even though the undescribed space holds apparent fragments of tropes and romance: piles of books like creamy white gangly bricks, diversions, naked legs, *now*, and the absence of them all in the necessity of a poetic life

Cont. Where was I? Oh yes, "… the reader then, *born*, unties the voice of self within the fabric of the poem…" Just as Mary, she says, THE OCEAN *walking*, giving birth to the context in which she creates, *birthing God*, giving birth to the context in which world creates. BIRTHING IMPLIES OCEAN &

LAND, *water and light*, how many times do I have to mention ropes and mooring? That is how I know I come from another surface, she says, yet the same visually presenting itself to you, *surface as surface*, two oceans kissing themselves in the end of each cycle (here cycle is to be understood as day), alas we forget *that the surface is that which forms ground*, and in order for ground to see itself, IT MUST PERCIEVE ITS SURFACE – and to ground oneself in this surface, we turn to the gaze of the other. Hence the exhibition of us (and the kissing and the whatnot). *Look at the ocean*: GOD IS WEAVING A SAIL, can't you see, for the sea to sail away, sail away to be, *and dolphins have invisible threads in their mouths*. But

don't get all effervescent on me, she says, THIS IS NOT
MERE L'ART POUR L'ART, *this is eschatology*, its beauty is merely residual, leftovers of universe, and I haven't even begun to assert anything of myself on it. IN LE GRANDE BLEU JAQUES TELLS US THAT YOU HAVE TO BE READY TO DIE AT THE BOTTOM OF THE OCEAN, *then the mermaids find you*, after this death. The vestimentary meaning of this: small changes in direction, *light lighter light water*, more, days within. YOU ARE THE
SALT OF THE EARTH, *the light of the world*, a nation seeking its inhabitants. The motion is already here, she says, but sometimes distracted by the billowing of body.
MICROMACRO, *we complete*, make the bed with sleep, fall asleep embedded in each other's brake from wakefulness. Sails, the ocean, *the ocean is sailing itself*, hence why you're present in my wetness

UN-FABRICATE myself, *through you*.
Once again: conscious or not, *CAN YOU POINT TOWARDS YOUR MIND?*, she asks while *in language* searching the pile for garments and lost memories to caress with words: alaeum or immemor, luxurious fabric or forgetfulness, *memories become physical and bloom out of bodies like metaphors of approach*, flowers and phenotypes. You cannot weave with a single thread, she says, INDEED – *two kinds are necessary*. When we weave with beauty: *small etheric nots are untying*, on epistemic meta-levels scarring is smoothened. EVERY WORD IN AFFECT, *despite promises of independency*, the adjective itself *here* loyal to the assessment of properties, as if the arbitrary flow of contingent things and strangers could ever touch us. THE ONLY THING IN THIS WORLD WE TRULY HAVE, she says, is the free ability to give ourselves to someone, *someone can take it* but then, seeing it is not given freely, it is not the same thing. Meaning someone can never take it, even

in immemor. *Shall I compare thee to a summer's day?* Now that you influence me with radiant things. HOW WE THEN USE OUR MEMORY: without a doubt carelessly, spots of golden-brown frost, *the autumn is old now*, autumn already written complete. The winter in anticipation calls for texture and yet it is known for the erasing of words. *In a metaphorical universe*, she says, THE
TEXT IS BUT THE ONE SURVIVING ELEMENT, here the page recalls the analogy with snow, *remember?* But the sheet, equally white and neutral, keeps the warmth when writing us, the page keeps poetry. YOU
ARE HERE MY DARLING YOU ARE SO UNBELIEVABLY HERE THAT IT IS OVERWHELMING, hence why we treat it poetically, with a parachute of poetry, to ease morning breaks and metamorphosis with metaphor and merciful words

Make ourselves quasi-obsolete, but always forgiven. THE TEXT IS FABRIC and weaves the history of your mind, *remolding*, she says. After you've read this, it is a part of your past, of your immaterial clothing. If you don't believe me then look at me and try calling me something else

THE LACK OF ABSENCE. I'm always met with images, she says, *even as the proposition of beauty refers to a pure image* and un-states itself, STILL IN THE
WORLD, still with the question I didn't expect to pronounce but later on, lost in my poetic naiveté. *Even rich in words*,
THE MIND IS A BLANK PAGE, white, the premise of words. Is the experience of beauty as such then an intrinsic value? COMPARABLE TO MIND, page, withdrawing sun and light, *seeing it cannot be considered either true or false.*
It simply is. A relentless redeeming approaches, returning heavens, foamy shiny white deliberations from seas gathering: THE SPACE INBETWEEN CLOUDS IS MY

BELOVED ABSENCE, *even these are clouds*, they look like words

I am because I can imagine my selfthinking, *thinking*, alive in the faint illumination of sketch, and with that imaginary thought I was created. I AM NOT ARROGANT ENOUGH TO PROPOSE NONDOUBT, she says, *nor am I semantically inclined to partake in such a performance*: on a thin day, a clear lake, shallow and potent enough to hold the body that holds my thoughts afloat, *floating*. ACTORS, said Descartes, taught to not let any embarrassment show on their faces, *put on a mask*, while, according to Yeats, the poet instead finds his mask in disappointment, the hero in defeat. *I shall do the same.* Then I can get a grip on this whole sign situation, clinch it like water, hold it like a pen to define my hands. WHEN I WAS IN PARIS THE LAST TIME I TRIED ON SEVERAL OCCASIONS TO

VISIT THE SHAKESPEARIAN BOOKSHOP BUT THE QEUE WAS HOURS LONG, *filled with people already there anecdotally*, to take a photo and put it on Instagram. This fabulation of reference and anecdote will kill the human soul, she remarked, *but for me?* I instead walked along the Seine and the art vendors and bought a copy of Salinger's *Raise High the Roof Beam, Carpenters* for 1€. THE INCLUSION OF THOUGHT SEEMS TO BE PROVOKED INTO EXISTANCE BY DISPLACEMENT, *because where are these people really supposed to be?*, &MORE IMPORTANTLY: *are they* spatially *losing their minds?*, the ones that don't read but line up for bookstores: a finger writing poems on the surface of water, thoughts filtered and then – *reflection*, I COME FORWARD MASKED, in this indiscreet autopoiesis of death, *now that honesty of self no longer signifies reflection.* VENUS IS A FISH, she says, and don't forget it, IF THERE IS AN AMATEUR

READER STILL LEFT IN THE WORLD, don't forget it: an answer rephrased, only in visceral fulfillment, a spark of self-contained sunshine, the poem of self is still weaving. HERE IS THE MANUAL, *she says*: 1. meet beginnings of thought with an end, 2. introduce yourself to new days with one last nightly breath. After all, she says, it is retrospection that affects the pen, that determines whether or not water slips through your fingers

TREES SPARKLE WITH THE DIVIDING OF CELLS, *an organic visual typesetting*, letters. Creation begins with *b*, she says, so that the poem always has a blank page, a premise safe from division and mimema. The mud here represents the mold of presumptive spaces, as if we've changed the aesthetic analogy: *IF I WALK BENEATH THE BLUE CANVAS*, bare feet on the newly cut green, muddy, *I touch both earth and heaven at the same time*. I must be assertive about this: I'm eternally falling in and out of poetry as both blank page and poetry. THERE IS NO ABSOLUTE NEGATION, the break in writing merely denotes blank page, *poetic*, and therefore eternal poetry. Meditation is but an unwritten page, she says, *but it nonetheless breathes poetry*: the preparation of new words, I AM HOLDING MY BREATH SHE SAYS, sunbathing in rain, thawing like winter turning into spring, *already in September*, dialectically rebellious. But the ground still carries warmth, she says curling up her naked feet, the park still unwriting itself

WE MUST WRAP THIS UP, *this poetics of apperception*, SOMEWHAT *INDOORS* and guessing, in subjects regarding oneself, one's guessing. A bee that slipped into the room is trying to get out, endlessly bumping up against the stained window. Ergo: I have started to question the preferences of bees, they don't seem to see the stains in my extrospective clouds, though my dirty windows. LIKE THEY IN SOME WAY COULD ALWAYS FLY TOWARDS THE UNCERTAIN *beyond*, even certainly against, bumping their small vibrating bodies against the invisible. This question now unravels from epistemology to ontology, she says, because clearly the bees know something: *can spotless then be referred to as perception*, borders within borders? SCENE: it is morning, and we are lying in bed looking out (I tell tales about day outside, but only outside). The gap that the bee doesn't seem to recollect is pointing inwards, cool air cleaning away the lull of night. A night that is over is unusable, she says as if disappointed to leave its definite arrest, found unsatisfied in the revelation of already fulfilled sleep, neither tired nor rested, albeit thrown out against world, nonetheless. DO WE SOMETIMES NEED TO ASK FOR STRUGGLE? Throw *ourselves* onto an invisible screen of need, *to regain comfort*, exhaust ourselves so we can actually rest. DO BEES CONSTRUCT ESCAPES TOWARDS ALLEVIATION, *call it the struggle with necessity*; is this what he is doing, the bee: *bumping himself tired again?* You go back, Jack, do it again, *wheels turnin' round and round*: is God only found in sleep, alas demanded by self-made strife? Don't argue with me and climb out of bed onto further beds until the day asks for commitment, *the bee is actually aiming for sky and space*, I'm guessing

Now I understand what you mean, she says, *how the magnificence of being isn't incorporated to the page of interpretation*, LIGHT IN A SECOND-HAND EXPERIENCE, *but into the page itself*, clean. AND THE SUMMER'S LEASE HATH ALL TO SHORT A DATE, we should with virtue shine therein, in the misrepresentation of darkness and latter seasons. Purple, dark streaming blue. *The imitated corpus can be a genre in the habitual sense of the term*, but here I'm withdrawing into autumns never alike. YET THE EVER-CHANGING GARMENTS OF SEASONS SEEMS TO NEVER CHANGE, like a text renewing itself against the same white page: of the ephemeral gules the anxious gravity, as haughtily ugly as the thornbush, but wait a minute, A CONTRACT BADLY FULFULLED IS NONETHELESS A PASTICHE, *I'm tempted to address waveforms and particles as such*, perhaps even speak more of water. I love to hear her speak, the ocean, well I know that music hath far more pleasing sound

BUT THE TROJAN POET IS ALIVE, *Cassandra was wrong* – he has risen, scratch the surface and you will find the elegiac. The duality of meaning, corresponding, THE SPACES-INBETWEEN ALREADY DECIDED, *weather and politics must certainly occupy the same*. With this gesture, she says, they have expropriated the world from the divine, *so what expectations are we befallen now?* The Bible tells us more than 350 times to not be afraid, but a self-excision seems to nonetheless be at hand; if the trope of pathos is to be invoked, then medicine here would be touch. DON'T WAKE ME UP I'M NOT DREAMING. In the Middle Ages, painters had the status of craftsmen who produced when commissioned. But who has requested our situation, *what has compelled the reader?*

"The artistic praxis includes not only the purely artistic skills, but also the awareness of what these skills are to communicate, that is, knowledge of the aesthetic and the theologico-political concepts which are a part of this praxis." *Aesthetic theory and practice in art history*, (Gunnar Danbolt).

Sure, but the plasticity of these requests is centered around you

LUNCHEON IN THE GRASS. *Quiet.*
Did you hear it? A star was formed out
of an imploding nebula, all the while
some were distracted by worldly illu-
sions, charming and sinister imitations
of light, we less, *here distracted by each other*,
at least producing light.
TO BECOME THE WIND
DOESN'T NECESSARILY
PROMOTE
A NATURAL UNREST, from the
bookshelf of persona a traveler reads
himself to peace. *Let's be blunt and materi-
alize an identity*, she says. Given the com-
plicated account of artistic production
that I've been tracing, this seems refresh-
ingly straightforward. On the face of
things, *let's give a face to our propria persona*.
A COMMON LANGUAGE, to do this
we need to deconstruct this image of me
here in nothing but a thong, not because
of shallow attempts of eroticism, but be-
cause this small piece of garment, parod-
ically vain, keeps the suspense of my to-
tal nakedness towards the other, *towards
you*. THE PERCEPTION OF
THE   WORLD

HANGS BY A SINGLE THREAD, *literally*, and your mind will dissolve in unlivable reality once I'm undressed. Schelling said that all effects of art are merely effects of nature for a person who has not attained a perception of art that is free, *but the wind nonetheless seeks limitations within the unlimited*. YOU ARE FREE, so deconstruct this image of me here in thong and cognitive architecture. We have already rediscovered us enough to always be inside, she says, and infinite interior, a poem within a poem, inwardly read. So, the question is rather how the question ought to be phrased: can you call the a priori knowledge of beauty for breakfast in the context of you eating me? On semiotic terms, clearly an excess of the plane of the signifier, *maybe less representation*: it is soon mid-day, the day outside the window looks bright and cool. If the reader of this book is to ever leave bed, she says, we need to go outdoors, maybe just to catch a breath of topos, renew the nostalgia of this textbed by leaving, *for a while*:

CALL IT AN ACHIEVEMENT OF A SPECULATIVE IDENTITY, we have to limit our wu wei to at least themes such as *interests* and *meetings*, even if the social life of others is merely to refer these back to ourselves. To put it sequentially: I slip out of this thong, your mind-world implodes – *I come*, we recollect each other, pick up the pieces and go for a shaky walk.

THE EXCESSIVE OBJECTS MIGHT WELL EXCITE A WISH TO BE INUNDATED, *but unless we rest in-between interests*, this promise will surely yield an anxiety of incorporation. Walking will dust off our beings, unless this custom becomes habitual, and we withdraw from the sublime. MY PLACE IS THE FRUITFUL BATHOS OF EXPERIENCE! And yet episodes of post-sensual melancholy seem awfully redundant. It is said that when Solomon married one of his wives, he sent his servant to pick out a gift that could make him happy in sad times and humble in happy times. The servant brought back a ring with the inscription:

THIS TOO SHALL PASS, even the refreshing act of non-sex, the fasting as such. If we return to the analogy of mountain edges and you coming, *this warm-wet climb up Mount Blanc*, then we can conclude its sublimity as factitious when arranged as an obligatory stop: *the clear and daily exposure blurs the sublime*, sometimes. What happens to the epitome of beauty if I stop reading, she asks, if I put away my verselets and my other pretty toys. BUT
THERE'S ALWAYS SOMETHING
NEW TO READ, *it's exhausting*, this never-exhausted economy of written things. Old kettles, old bottles and the shedding of thong: *I must lay down where all the ladders start*, the subtext of this concludes the Latin language, it cannot be helped: *res* means *thing*, in this thing of ours, but also denotes a real estate of sorts, this reality thing of ours. But in the world-construct, reality outside seems neutralized. *To be rebellious to worlds by simply being in nature*, in autumn, the alchemy of arbitrary air: I HERE ENACT

THE ROLE OF RECONQUISTA-DOR, a Viking of my own lands: *let the end commence*, and now we wander in the means, the dark green park behind the library. But beyond the hills? Eh? Perhaps it's still green? Eh? FLORA! POMONA! CERES! It is clear that it is too cold outside for a luncheon in the grass

MOBILE BEDS, *as if boat*. If they hadn't gone backwards for ideas, she says, we might not have intercepted the regression with the bed of each other, *as if the question didn't already hold the answer*, floating on ifs as if disjunctive. And by the way, do we have time to entertain hypothetical ignorance? REAL FREEDOM IS SOMETHING OF THE MIND, *in the soul*, SOMETHING LAID UP IN HEAVEN. Establish, move on. The favorable thing with their regression, she says, is that I can remain in bed and still be on my way. There are imitations of an iconography that cannot be clearly interpreted, *sure*, BUT THE PLANET IS NONETHELESS TRAVELING, we always have first row seats. You don't have to understand everything, just let it go. It is still warm herein, cold outside where life is supposed to mean greater things. It certainly has something to do with the appropriate portrayal of the mind-world, she says, but I cannot take seriously that which water doesn't reflect. WHEREVER CAPRICE TAKES ME, *the I amble alone*. Is planet earth really

God's flaneur, *floating*? If the world is to be likened with mind and space with water, then how do I put this

(Someone somewhere in something slipping my memory wrote: *this boat, like a bed, espouses sleep.* But here it espouses awakedness, not me sleeping, and yet a form of sleep, addressed as me awake. But even though I could sense the metaphor of sun and beauty in Tolstoy's Anna Karenina when I wrote this, chiasm and rhythm and so on, this affiliation will not be explored as such, *although important to point out in terms of anchoring and aesthetics*: YOU ARE LIKE THE WOMAN LIKENED TO SUN IN TOLSTOY'S ANNA KARENINA, *so beautiful a thing me cannot look directly at further definitions*, completely inalienable and yet somewhat removed. I am awake now, you see, and still obviously driven out of myself, for a moment dreaming, advantageously so: AFTER THIS LONG EXCURSION INTO THE

MORE DISTANT REGIONS OF REALITY, *let us surely return to images closer to daydream*, reality)

IN THE OCEAN OF SPACE, the conceptual writer is God, *the pen is the sun*. Aaron threw his stick on the ground, and it became a serpent, but here the perennial character is the event of meaningfulness itself. WHEN I TRY
TO TYPE
ALCHEMY
ON MY PHONE IT CHANGES TO SCHEMA, as some sort of ontogenetic prophecy of form. "Will there be any artforms left when we see that artforms are all really metaphors and AI has exceeded us as medium?," is a question to unpoetically demanding to ask, but anyway, here's my prophecy: the only thing left will be writing. Let me see, she says, *how can I put this?*, this thing that I am trying to put. Maybe it has to do with just that, the sheer distance, when it comes to neglecting the obvious and make that

which is closest seem furthest away. I AM PUTTING ON MY CLOTHES AT SOME POINT, just as the soul once dressed in body. We must un-fabricate, and then maybe the stars in sky appear in apparition again, closer than the lights from the next-door town: THAT EVEN IF THE CLOUDS PASS THOUSANDS OF FEET ABOVE OUR HEADS, like unhyphened fragments of a story still whole, *it is yet closest to the skin that the sun is missing.* I am actually here now, she says when nights befall us, *like the light from a distant star*, in this scheme I happened to be indoors starlight

www.ingramcontent.com/pod-product-compliance
Lightning Source LLC
Chambersburg PA
CBHW052149070526
44585CB00017B/2040